VIRGINIA

Janice Parker

Published by Weigl Publishers Inc.
123 South Broad Street, Box 227
Mankato, MN 56002
USA
Web site: http://www.weigl.com

Library of Congress Cataloging-in-Publication Data available upon
request from the publisher. Fax: (507) 388-2746 for the attention of the
Publishing Records Department.

ISBN 1-930954-94-8

Printed in the United States of America
1 2 3 4 5 6 7 8 9 10   05 04 03 02 01

Editor
Michael Lowry
Copy Editor
Diana Marshall
Designers
Warren Clark
Terry Paulhus
Layout
Susan Kenyon
Photo Researcher
Angela Lowen

Photograph Credits
Every reasonable effort has been made to trace ownership and to obtain
permission to reprint copyright material. The publishers would be
pleased to have any errors or omissions brought to their attention so
that they may be corrected in subsequent printings.

Cover: Young Soldier (Bruce Roberts); Peanuts (Corel Corporation); **Corel Corporation:** pages 3M, 10T, 11B, 23T, 23B; **Defense Visual Information Center:** page 15; **Digital Stock Corporation:** page 11T; **Library of Virginia:** pages 16T, 16B, 17T, 17B, 18T, 18B, 19T; **PhotoDisc Corporation:** page 14T; **Photofest:** pages 3B, 25T, 25B; **Bruce Roberts:** pages 12BL, 14B; **Virginia Tourism Corporation:** pages 3T, 4T, 4BL, 4BR, 6T, 6BL, 6BR, 7T, 7B, 8T, 8B, 9T, 9B, 10B, 12T, 12BR, 13T, 13B, 19B, 20T, 21T, 21BL, 21BR, 22T, 22B, 24T, 24BL, 24BR, 26T, 26B, 27T, 27B, 28T, 28B, 29L, 29R.

CONTENTS

Virginia is known as the "Mother of States" because eight other states were formed from its land.

INTRODUCTION

Virginia secured its place in United States history when it became one of the original thirteen states. The state's nicknames—"The Birthplace of Presidents" and "The Birthplace of a Nation"— reveal that Virginia's historical figures participated in the creation of the United States. Virginians George Washington, Thomas Jefferson, James Madison, and James Monroe helped found the country during their terms as the first, third, fourth, and fifth presidents of the United States.

Before becoming president of the United States, George Washington was **commander in chief** of the Continental Army during the American Revolution. In 1787, he led the meeting of the **Constitutional Convention**, which drafted the Constitution of the United States. Washington was **unanimously** elected the first president of the United States. He was nicknamed "Father of His Country" for his work in creating the country's system of government.

QUICK FACTS

Virginia's state flag has been flown since the 1830s. The flag features the state seal against a blue background and was officially adopted in 1930.

The state's official name is the Commonwealth of Virginia. Three other states are considered commonwealth states— Kentucky, Massachusetts, and Pennsylvania. Commonwealth is an honorary title meaning "for the common good."

During the early 1800s, the steamboat was the fastest and cheapest method of transporting goods in Virginia.

QUICK FACTS

Close to 43,000
passengers use the Ronald Reagan Washington National Airport each day. The airport is situated on the west bank of the Potomac River.

Virginia has about
70,000 miles of highway.

More than 5.8 million
motor vehicles are registered in Virginia.

Richmond has been
the state capital of Virginia since 1780. Williamsburg was the state capital from 1699 to 1780, and Jamestown was the state capital from 1607 to 1699.

On June 25, 1788,
Virginia became the tenth state to join the Union.

Getting There

Virginia is located on the eastern coast of the United States. It is bordered by Maryland to the northeast, Kentucky and West Virginia to the west, and North Carolina and Tennessee to the south.

The state has eleven commercial airports, including three international airports. The Washington Dulles International Airport is the fourth-busiest airport in the United States for **transatlantic** air service. The airport serves about 20 million passengers each year.

One of the best ways to travel to, and around, Virginia is by automobile. Major highways and smaller scenic roads provide access to all parts of the state. Six interstate highways run through Virginia—the I-64, I-66, I-77, I-81, I-85, and I-95. The Chesapeake Bay Bridge-Tunnel connects Virginia's Eastern Shore with the state's mainland. Ferry service is also available across James River and Chesapeake Bay.

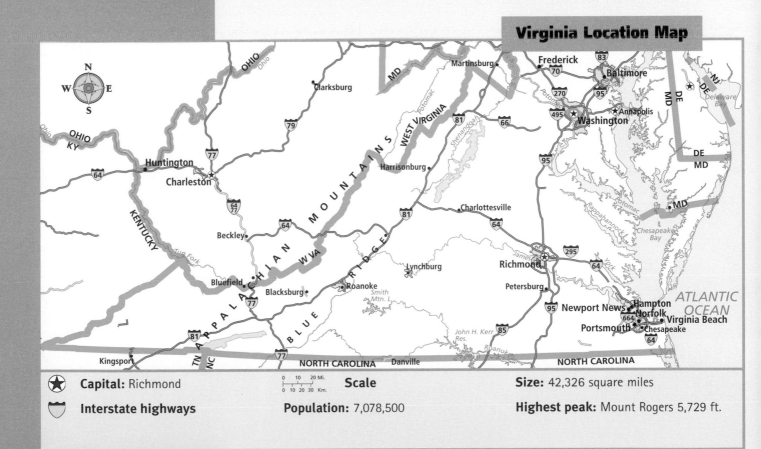

Virginia Location Map

★ **Capital:** Richmond

🛡 **Interstate highways**

Scale
0 10 20 Mi.
0 10 20 30 Km.

Population: 7,078,500

Size: 42,326 square miles

Highest peak: Mount Rogers 5,729 ft.

During the American Revolution, many Virginians fought for independence from Great Britain.

QUICK FACTS

Virginia is nicknamed "The Old Dominion" because of its loyalty to Charles I of England during the English Civil War (1642-1648).

Virginia was named for Elizabeth I, the "Virgin Queen," of England.

The American foxhound is the state dog. George Washington first brought foxhounds into Virginia to hunt foxes.

Virginia played a crucial role in the American Revolution. It was Virginian Thomas Jefferson who was responsible for writing the Declaration of Independence, which announced the independence of the thirteen colonies from Great Britain. In 1781, the final battle of the American Revolution was fought on Virginian soil, in Yorktown. During the Siege of Yorktown, American and French troops, led by General George Washington surrounded the British, who were led by Lord Cornwallis. The British forces surrendered after twenty days, and the war was officially ended in 1783 with the signing of the **Treaty of Paris**.

In April 1861, Virginia decided to leave the Union, and Richmond served as the capital of the Confederacy from May 1861 to April 1865. The Confederacy won many important battles in Virginia, including the first and second battles of Bull Run, Jackson's Valley Campaign, and the battles of Fredericksburg and Chancellorsville. The Confederate Army surrendered to Union troops under the command of General Ulysses S. Grant at Appomattox, Virginia, on April 9, 1865.

Virginia was the site of more than half of the 4,000 battles fought during the American Civil War.

Many of Virginia's rivers can be navigated by small boats, such as canoes.

Virginia's rich soils have helped to make agriculture a primary industry. The tobacco industry was crucial to the success of the Virginia colony. Settlers in the Virginia colony began to grow tobacco in 1612. Tobacco became such an important moneymaking crop that without it, the colony may not have survived. In the twentieth century, the manufacturing of tobacco products was an essential part of the state's economy.

A large part of Virginia's population lives in the Washington, D.C. **metropolitan** area. The nation's capital was formed in 1790 from parts of Virginia and Maryland. Today, Virginia's close association with the national capital has an enormous impact on the state's economy and culture. Government offices and military bases in Virginia provide jobs for nearly 20 percent of the state's population.

QUICK FACTS

The official salute to the flag is "I salute the flag of Virginia, with reverence and patriotic devotion to the 'Mother of States and Statesmen,' which it represents—the 'Old Dominion,' where liberty and independence were born." The salute was adopted in 1954.

The Arlington National Cemetery is the federal burial ground for more than 240,000 veterans, and important political leaders. The cemetery contains the Tomb of the Unknown Soldier, which is guarded 24 hours a day, and the grave of John F. Kennedy, which is marked by an eternal flame.

The first peanuts grown in the United States were grown in Virginia.

About 25 percent of Virginians live in the countryside.

On average, the Shenandoah Valley receives 25 inches of snow every year.

LAND AND CLIMATE

The state of Virginia is triangular in shape. It includes an area known as the Eastern Shore on the Delmarva Peninsula. The Eastern Shore is separated from the mainland by Chesapeake Bay. Extending inland from the coast is the Coastal Plain, a flat and swampy region. The Piedmont to the west of the Coastal Plain is characterized by fertile soils. The Blue Ridge region is made up of mountains that form a ridge crossing the western tip of the state. The ridge is part of the Appalachian Ridge and extends from West Virginia to North and South Carolina.

While Virginia generally has hot, humid summers and mild, wet winters, the climate varies throughout the state. Southeastern Virginia, near the coast, has a mild climate with very little snowfall. The average January temperature for this region is 40° Fahrenheit, while the average July temperature is 78°F. The northwestern part of the state has colder winters.

The only way to reach Tangier Island, in Chesapeake Bay, is by boat or small plane.

QUICK FACTS

Virginia is the thirty-fifth largest state in the country. It covers an area of 42,326 square miles. Virginia has 112 miles of coastline.

Mount Rogers is the highest point in Virginia, with an altitude of 5,729 feet.

Some of the major rivers in Virginia are the James River, Rappahannock River, Potomac River, and Shenandoah River.

More than three-quarters of the forestland in Virginia is privately owned.

QUICK FACTS

Natural Tunnel, near Duffield, is 100 feet high and 850 feet long and passes through a mountain ridge to a canyon. The tunnel was created by a river that once ran through the canyon.

The state has about 49,000 miles of rivers and streams. The state also has approximately 450 lakes.

The growing season in Virginia ranges from 150 to 230 days. In the southeastern part of the state, the growing season begins in late March and lasts until the middle of November. The growing season in the west begins at the end of April and continues until early October.

Much of Virginia is covered with fertile soils. The southern Coastal Plain contains **bog** soils, which are rich in minerals.

NATURAL RESOURCES

Forests cover more than 60 percent of Virginia. Most of the trees are hardwood species but softwoods such as the loblolly pine and yellow poplar are also common. Many of Virginia's forests are secondary-growth forests, which means they have grown in areas previously cleared by logging. Today, most logging occurs in central and southern parts of the Piedmont region. In an effort to preserve the state's forests, large sections of farmland have recently been replanted with trees.

Virginia has an abundance of mineral resources, including clay, coal, gravel, and limestone. Coal is the state's most important mineral. About 37 million tons of coal are produced each year. Virginia is the only state that produces kyanite, a mineral used to make bricks. The production of minerals contributes nearly $670 million to the state's economy every year.

Virginia's fertile soils produce excellent grassland for grazing horses.

PLANTS AND ANIMALS

There are more than 400 different species of geranium.

Hardwood trees, such as hickories, maples, and white and red oaks, are abundant in Virginia forests. Other trees commonly found in the state include evergreens, white pines, sycamores, and willows. In the wetlands, tupelos, bald cypresses, and swamp oaks grow. Dogwood can be found throughout most of the state, while azaleas, mountain laurels, and rhododendrons are common in the mountain regions.

Wildflowers, such as windflowers, geraniums, asters, and trilliums, add color to the Virginian countryside. The Virginia Native Plant Society was founded in 1982 to help conserve plants that are native to the state. The society also chooses a wildflower of the year. One popular wildflower is the trailing arbutus, commonly known as the mayflower. The mayflower is a small, evergreen shrub that grows in forested areas. Pinkish-white flowers appear on the plant in early spring.

The brown-eyed Susan is a common plant in Virginia. Its scientific name, *Rudbeckia triloba*, means "thin-leaved cornflower."

QUICK FACTS

The dogwood was adopted as the official state flower of Virginia in 1918. In 1956, the dogwood was also declared the state tree. The flowers on a dogwood tree are actually groupings of colorful leaves.

According to the United States Fish and Wildlife Service, there are thirteen species of plants in Virginia that are either **endangered** or **threatened**. These include the eastern prairie fringed orchid and the Virginia round-leaf birch.

Humpback whales follow migration paths that lead them past the coast of Virginia.

Many species of whales can be found off the coast of Virginia, including humpback and fin whales.

Virginia's official state bird is the cardinal. The brook trout is the state fish, the tiger swallowtail butterfly is the state insect, and the oyster is the state shell.

Three species of venomous snakes can be found in Virginia—the timber rattlesnake, the northern copperhead, and the eastern cottonmouth.

Fifty-nine Virginian animal species are on the United States Fish and Wildlife Service's Threatened and Endangered Species list, including three species of bats and several species of sea turtles.

While many large mammals once lived in Virginia, only the black bear and the white-tailed deer still roam the state. Smaller mammals are more abundant. Beavers, muskrats, skunks, otters, foxes, and raccoons make their homes in Virginia. Common reptiles and **amphibians** include the box turtle and the bullfrog. More than thirty species of snakes, such as the eastern garter snake, live in Virginia.

Virginia is located along the path of the Atlantic Flyway. The flyway is a route for migrating birds that runs along the eastern coast of North America. Migrating ducks and geese take advantage of the many rivers and marshes in the state. During summer, warblers and orioles live in Virginia. Nuthatches and woodpeckers live in the state's forests, while gulls, herons, and bitterns reside around lakes and ponds. Birds of prey that live in the state include the bald eagle, the peregrine falcon, and the osprey.

Bullfrogs are the largest frogs in North America, measuring up to 8 inches in length. Bullfrogs can be found throughout Virginia.

Visitors to Assateague Island can enjoy 37 miles of surf and sand.

TOURISM

The beauty of Virginia Beach once prompted an early explorer to exclaim, "Heaven and Earth never agreed better to frame a place for man's habitations than Virginia." Today, Virginia Beach is not only the largest city in the state, but is also one of the most popular resorts on the East Coast. Approximately 2.5 million tourists visit Virginia Beach every year.

One of Virginia's most treasured sites is Monticello—the home of Thomas Jefferson. For more than forty years, Jefferson built and rebuilt the house into one of the most impressive homes in the world. Another popular attraction is George Washington's boyhood home near Falmouth.

Tourists are also drawn to Virginia's many historic attractions. Battlefields from the American Revolution and the American Civil War are scattered across the state, including Yorktown, the site of the final battle of the American Revolution.

QUICK FACTS

The Virginia Zoo, in Norfolk, was founded as a park in 1899 and began to collect animals the following year. Today, the zoo has about 340 animals.

More than 4 million visitors come to Williamsburg each year. Many of the village's buildings and streets have been restored to their eighteenth-century splendor.

Monticello is the only house in the country listed on the United Nations' World Heritage List.

The birthplace of George Washington, in Westmoreland County, has been attracting visitors from around the world since 1815.

Commercial fishing in Virginia has an annual catch of 460 million pounds.

INDUSTRY

Agriculture is the largest moneymaking industry in Virginia. It is responsible for about 11 percent of the **Gross State Product** of Virginia. Each year, the state earns more than $35 billion from agricultural sales. Virginia is home to about 50,000 farms, which cover 8.8 million acres of land, or about 34 percent of the total land area. Agriculture creates close to 235,800 jobs, which account for almost 10 percent of all jobs in the state. Principal farm products include **broiler chickens**, chicken eggs, cattle, greenhouse or nursery goods, milk, tobacco, turkeys, and peanuts. About half of Virginia's farmland is used to grow crops, while the rest is forest or pasture.

Chesapeake Bay provides Virginia with many different types of fish. Commercial fishing in Virginia contributes more than $108 million to the state's economy each year. This makes it one of the top ten ranking commercial fishing states in the country. Crab and oyster production is high in Virginia. Clams, flounders, scallops, and striped bass are also important to commercial fishing in the state.

Virginia's 48,000 farms cover about one-third of the state.

QUICK FACTS

The News Shipbuilding and Dry Dock Company, in Newport News, is the world's largest privately owned shipyard. The company employs 17,000 people and has built more than 800 naval and commercial ships.

Leading industries in Virginia include publishing and printing, and the manufacturing of paper products, electrical equipment, and automobiles.

Chemical products are Virginia's most valuable manufactured goods.

GOODS AND SERVICES

Virginia's leading manufactured goods are tobacco and chemical products. Food, clothing, transportation equipment, furniture, wood products, and electrical equipment are also important manufactured goods. Virginia's top ten exports include tobacco products, and crops such as corn, wheat, and soybeans.

The federal government employs many Virginians and is essential to the state's economy. Several Virginian cities and counties are part of the Washington, D.C. metropolitan area. About 23,000 military and **civilian** employees work in the Pentagon in Arlington. The Pentagon is the headquarters of the United States Department of Defense and is one of the largest office buildings in the world.

QUICK FACTS

On September 11, 2001, a hijacked commercial airplane crashed into the Pentagon causing part of it to collapse. More than 180 people were killed. The crash was part of a terrorist attack on the United States, which also resulted in the destruction of the twin towers of the World Trade Center in New York City. The Pentagon quickly recovered from the attack to coordinate the fight against terrorism. On October 7, 2001, the United States and its allies began air strikes against terrorist camps in Afghanistan.

The Pentagon has 17.5 miles of hallways. Fortunately, the Pentagon's unique five-sided design means that it only takes 7 minutes to walk between any two points in the building.

Virginia is home to nearly 122,000 military personnel, including 41,600 in the Navy and Marine Corps.

Virginia's first newspaper was the *Gazette*, which began publication in 1736, in Williamsburg. There are 33 daily newspapers, 29 television stations, and 271 radio stations in Virginia.

When the Syms Free School in Hampton was founded in 1634, it became the first school in the United States.

All Virginian children between the ages of 5 and 18 years must attend school.

More than 362,000 students are enrolled in colleges and universities in Virginia.

Many important military bases are located in Virginia, including the world's largest naval station at Norfolk. The Marine Corps Base in Quantico is where all U.S. marines receive their basic education. The state's military facilities cover a total area of about 450 square miles.

The Library of Virginia, in Richmond, contains the **archives** of the Commonwealth of Virginia. The library assists the public, other libraries, and the government with reference and research questions. The library's collections focus on the history, culture, and government of Virginia. The library also collects works by all Virginia authors in the Virginia Center for the Book.

Thomas Jefferson founded the University of Virginia in 1819. The university awards approximately 5,300 degrees each year. The U.S. News and World Report ranked the University of Virginia the top public university in the country, tied with the University of California, at Berkeley.

Founded in 1916, Langley Air Force Base employs more than 11,000 people.

FIRST NATIONS

When European settlers first met Chief Powhatan, he looked so young and strong that they could not believe he was nearly 60 years old.

Archeological remains reveal that Paleo-Indians lived in the Virginia region about 10,000 years ago. These early peoples used tools made of stone and relied mainly on hunting for their food. About 3,000 years ago, some groups began to settle in villages. They hunted, fished, and grew crops, such as corn and squash. They also began to grow tobacco, make ceramic pottery, such as bowls, and trade with nearby groups.

Archeologists believe that there were at least 10,000 Native Americans in the region by the 1600s. Various groups spoke different languages, which belonged to three main language groups. The first European settlers came into contact with citizens of the Powhatan Confederacy, who lived near the coast. Powhatan was the ruler of about thirty groups in the confederacy. The relationship between the European settlers and the Powhatans took a turn for the worse when violence erupted. In 1613, the English colonists captured the ruler's daughter, Pocahontas. Pocahontas eventually married an English settler, John Rolfe.

QUICK FACTS

The Pamunkey and Mattaponi reservations in Virginia were the first Native-American reservations in the United States.

The marriage of Pocahontas to John Rolfe brought peace to the area for close to 8 years. Fighting resumed between the Powhatans and the English after the death of Pocahontas in 1617.

Pocahontas died in England before she and her husband could return to Virginia.

The population of the Powhatan Confederacy in the 1600s was about 12,000.

EXPLORERS AND MISSIONARIES

English explorer John Cabot is believed to have been the first European to see Virginia, when he reached North America in 1497. In 1524, Italian explorer Giovanni da Verrazzano explored Virginia's coast for France.

In 1607, three ships carrying 144 men from the Virginia Company of London traveled from England to North America. The Virginia Company of London was created to settle Virginia. When the company arrived in the region, they founded a settlement called Jamestown. The company settled the region with hopes of opening new areas for trade, converting the region's peoples to Christianity, and preventing the Spanish from taking over the land. The colonists suffered through some difficult periods of drought and many starved to death. Although the Virginia Company sent more men and supplies to the colony, thousands of settlers died. The colony's first governor, Thomas West, Baron de la Warr, was appointed in 1609. His deputy governor, Sir Thomas Gates, arrived in Jamestown in 1610 to find only sixty settlers. Just as the men were about to abandon the settlement, Governor West arrived and took control of the colony. Gradually, life in the settlement began to improve.

Thomas West was governor of Virginia for only a short period of time. In 1611, he returned to England to plead for the colony and did not survive the journey back.

Pocahontas became good friends with one of Virginia's earliest explorers, John Smith, after she saved his life.

William Berkeley became the governor of Virginia in 1624.

QUICK FACTS

In 1644, the Powhatans attacked the Virginia colony, killing about 500 settlers. In a peace agreement, the Native Peoples agreed to move north of the James and York Rivers, and eventually moved westward.

After the death of Pocahontas and her father Powhatan, the Powhatans killed about 350 colonists, including all six council members, during what is called "The Great Massacre."

The House of Burgesses, a branch of Virginia's early government, was the first elected body in North America.

EARLY SETTLERS

John Rolfe, a colonist who came to the Virginia colony in 1610, began to grow a type of tobacco from the West Indies that had a pleasant taste. Native Peoples had being using tobacco as a medicine and in ceremonies for at least 2,000 years. Virginia colonists began to grow tobacco and export it to England. The new, milder tobacco that Rolfe cultivated became very popular in England and the rest of Europe. Rolfe is responsible for Virginia's long and successful history with tobacco.

Based mainly upon the success of the tobacco industry, the Virginia colony began to thrive. The colonists were allowed to grow crops for their own profit, which encouraged many settlers to work hard. By 1619, the colony had its own government, with a two-chambered legislature. In 1620, women were sent to the colony. In 1624, Virginia became a royal colony.

Jamestown was the first successful English colony in North America.

The location of Jamestown was chosen so that it would be secure from Spanish attacks.

By 1641, close to 7,500 European settlers lived in Virginia. About three-quarters of these settlers had arrived as either apprentices or servants. Many of them became farmers. The colony also included about 250 Africans. European men were the only citizens allowed to vote.

In 1676, a group of settlers led by English aristocrat and colonist, Nathaniel Bacon, rose in rebellion against the Virginia government, in what is known as "Bacon's Rebellion." The group was angered by many of the governor's policies. They disliked Governor William Berkeley's refusal to call elections, his lack of a plan to combat attacks from Native Peoples, and his favoritism of new wealthy colonists. The rebels forced Berkeley to leave and then destroyed Jamestown. After Bacon died unexpectedly, Berkeley returned, reclaimed power, and hanged many of the rebels without trials.

By the beginning of the eighteenth century, about 58,000 people lived in Virginia. The tobacco industry continued to grow, and the colony thrived. Just prior to the American Revolution, the state's population had grown to almost 120,000 citizens.

Some historians consider Virginia's Thanksgiving in 1619 to be the first Thanksgiving in North America. The pilgrims did not celebrate their first Thanksgiving until 1621.

POPULATION

The population of Lexington is about 7,100.

Virginia has a population of approximately 7 million citizens. About 72 percent of the population is of European descent. Many people have British, German, or Irish heritage. Nearly one-quarter of the population is younger than 18 years of age, and about 6.5 percent is younger than 5 years of age. More than 11 percent of the population is 65 years and older.

Most Virginians—nearly eight out of every ten—live in metropolitan areas. Some of these areas fall entirely within the state, while others are part of the Washington, D.C. metropolitan area. There are almost 2.6 million households in the state, and about 68 percent of Virginians are homeowners. Approximately 86 percent of Virginians over the age of 25 years are high school graduates. Nearly 32 percent of the state's citizens have a university degree. The average household income is $40,000, which is $3,000 more than the national average.

QUICK FACTS

The population of Virginia is expected to reach 8.47 million people by the year 2025.

The population density in Virginia is about 178 people per square mile. The average **population density** of the United States is about 77 people per square mile.

Virginia is the twelfth most populated state. Half of the total population of the United States lives within about 500 miles of the state capital.

Virginia Cultural Groups

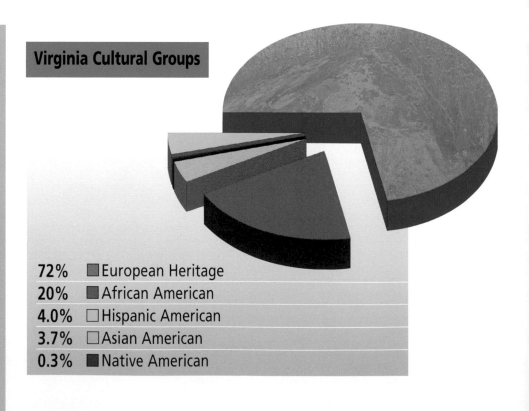

72%	■	European Heritage
20%	■	African American
4.0%	☐	Hispanic American
3.7%	☐	Asian American
0.3%	■	Native American

The White House of the Confederate States was located in Richmond from 1861 to 1865.

QUICK FACTS

Virginia is divided into 95 counties. The state has 40 cities, each run by an elected city manager and council, and 189 towns.

Virginia sends eleven representatives and two senators to the United States Congress, and has thirteen presidential electoral votes.

Virginia's state seal features Virtus the goddess of virtue. Virtus holds two swords. Her left foot stands on a figure, representing tyranny, lying on the ground. The seal was adopted in 1776.

POLITICS AND GOVERNMENT

Virginia is governed under its state constitution. The constitution divides the Virginia government into three branches—the executive, legislative, and judicial. The head of the executive branch is the state governor, who is elected to a four-year term. The governor has the power to approve or **veto** state laws. Other elected executive officials include the lieutenant governor and the attorney general, who both serve four-year terms.

The state legislature is called the General Assembly, and consists of a House of Delegates, with 100 members, and a Senate, with 40 members. Delegates are elected for two-year terms, while senators are elected for four-year terms. The General Assembly creates and changes the laws.

The judicial branch is the state's court system, which is made up of four levels of courts. The highest court is the Supreme Court.

The General Assembly meets in the Capitol in Richmond. The Capitol was designed by Thomas Jefferson, and was first used in 1788.

CULTURAL GROUPS

A re-creation of Virginia's first Thanksgiving takes place at the Berkeley Plantation every November.

Many of the festivals held throughout Virginia celebrate the state's long history and the lives of the early European settlers. The Frontier Culture Museum has exhibits that show what life was like for the early European settlers in Virginia. The Virginia First Thanksgiving Festival is held each year and features re-creations of the original celebration, including crafts, music, and plenty of food.

Native-American culture is celebrated throughout Virginia. Clarksville is the site of the Annual Native American Heritage Festival and Powwow held in May. It features Native-American arts, songs, and dances. Visitors can sample Native-American foods, such as buffalo burgers and fried bread. The festival also features traditional drumming and crafts, bow and arrow construction, and jewelry making.

The Frontier Culture Museum, in Staunton, is dedicated to preserving the culture of early colonial groups such the Scottish, Irish, and Germans.

Between 1990 and 2000, the Indian population in Virginia increased by 138 percent.

The first Africans arrived in the Virginia colony in 1619. During African-American Heritage Month each February, Virginians remember the history of African Americans in the state, and the African-American contributions to the early history of the nation. The Pocahontas State Park holds the African American History Festival, which celebrates the roots of African-American history in Virginia, from the early 1600s to the present day.

People from India and Pakistan make up the largest Asian group in Virginia, with a population of more than 48,800. In the 1990s, many Indian immigrants came to Virginia on a new six-year work visa allowing foreigners with special skills, such as computer skills, to come to the United States. The Vietnamese population in Virginia is also growing quickly. There are about 37,000 people from Vietnam in the state.

QUICK FACTS

Virginian African Americans received full **emancipation** in 1865.

The AFR'AM Fest, a week-long festival held in Norfolk, is a celebration of African-American accomplishments. This popular festival features African-American dance, music, plays, and educational exhibits.

Virginia is home to the largest Vietnamese community on the East Coast.

One of the largest Filipino communities in the United States is found in the Norfolk region.

It is an Indian custom to provide guests with offering bowls. Each bowl contains a different offering, such as flowers, fruit, or water.

The Virginia Museum of Fine Arts contains artwork from ancient Egypt.

ARTS AND ENTERTAINMENT

The arts have a long history of support in Virginia. In 1934, the Virginia Museum of Fine Arts, in Richmond, became the first state museum in the country dedicated to the arts. Ballet companies, symphony orchestras, opera companies, and theater groups also thrive in Virginia.

Virginia has produced many well-known writers. In the mid-nineteenth century, Edgar Allan Poe became popular for his poetry, short stories, and essays. Born in Boston, Poe was raised in Virginia and briefly attended the University of Virginia. Writer Tom Wolfe was born in Richmond in 1931. He wrote the acclaimed novels *The Bonfire of the Vanities* and *The Right Stuff*.

QUICK FACTS

The Barter Theatre, in Abingdon, allowed actors to perform in exchange for food during the Great Depression.

The Virginia Symphony was founded in 1920 and performs more than 140 concerts each year.

In 1922, the Edgar Allan Poe Museum opened in Richmond to document and celebrate the writer's life.

Theatre Virginia, in Richmond, has been staging plays for more than 45 years.

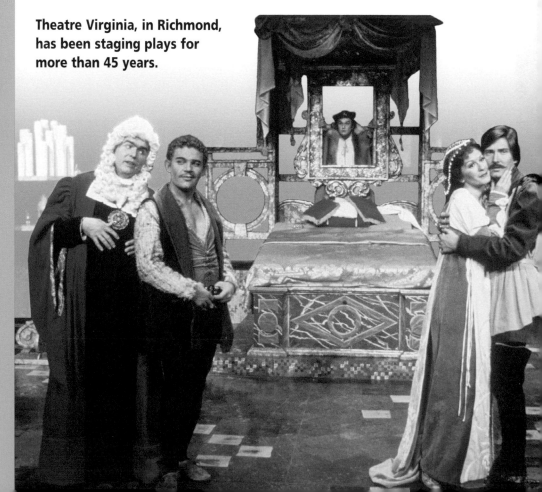

In 1995, an album of Patsy Cline's greatest hits sold 6 million copies.

Two talented female vocalists were born in Newport News. Born in 1917, Ella Fitzgerald is often referred to as the "First Lady of Song." Her career lasted for 60 years, and she has influenced countless other jazz singers and musicians. Born in 1918, Pearl Bailey was known for her bold stage performances and her work in nightclubs on Broadway and in Hollywood.

Virginia has also produced many renowned country and western music singers and performers. Patsy Cline was born in Winchester in 1932. She began singing as a young child and reached the top of the country music charts in 1962. She died the following year in a plane crash, but her music has had a great impact on other country music performers. Cline was the first woman to be **inducted** into the Country Music Hall of Fame. Country music performers Junc Carter Cash and Roy Clark are also native Virginians.

QUICK FACTS

Ella Fitzgerald recorded more than 2,000 songs and sold more than 40 million albums.

Katie Couric, who became coanchor on *The Today Show* in 1991, was born in Arlington.

Sibling actors Shirley MacLaine and Warren Beatty were born in Richmond.

Willa Cather, who lived from 1873 to 1947, was a journalist and novelist who won the Pulitzer Prize in 1923 for her novel *One of Ours*. Cather was born in Back Creek Valley.

During her career, Ella Fitzgerald won thirteen Grammy Awards.

There are many clubs and organizations for avid cyclists in Virginia.

SPORTS

Virginia's rivers, lakes, forests, mountains, and coastal areas offer a variety of recreational opportunities. Camping, hiking, hunting, boating, and fishing are popular in the state, especially in the national forests and state parks. The eastern coast is lined with beaches that offer various water sports. Boating is popular on the many lakes in the state, especially Buggs Island Lake and Smith Mountain Lake. The James, Shenandoah, and Maury Rivers are popular sites for white-water canoeing. Sections of the James River have Class 4 rapids, which are the most challenging and exciting. Fishers need licenses to catch the more than twenty-five species of freshwater fish in the state. Virginia is also considered one of the best places in the world for saltwater fishing.

Hikers, bicyclers, and horseback riders can take advantage of railroad trails that are no longer used. The New River Trail is a 52-mile rail bed between Galax and Pulaski, while the Virginia Creeper Trail, between Abingdon and Whitetop, is 34 miles long. Hikers also use the 450-mile portion of the Appalachian Trail that winds through Virginia.

The Shenandoah River is a popular destination for canoeists.

QUICK FACTS

Virginia is home to some of the best golf resorts in the nation and almost 200 daily-fee golf courses. Golf is played year-round throughout the state. The Homestead's Cascades is considered one of the best courses in the country.

Legendary golfers Sam Snead and Curtis Strange are Virginians. Snead was born near Hot Springs, while Strange was born in Norfolk.

About 300 miles of trails and ten swimming beaches make Virginia's thirty-four state parks and twenty-nine natural areas popular locations for recreation. More than 6.3 million people visit the state parks each year. Seashore State Park is the busiest, with 1.2 million visitors each year.

The Massanutten Resort, near Harrisonburg, features a snowboard park.

Downhill skiing in Virginia is available at four resorts—the Homestead, Bryce, Massanutten, and Wintergreen. Bryce Resort, in the Shenandoah Valley, also offers grass skiing during the summer. Grass skiing is skiing on grass using skates instead of skis. The sport was invented in Europe as a way to help skiers continue their training during summer months. Another new summer sport at Bryce Resort is mountain boarding. Mountain boarding is like snowboarding on wheels. It combines aspects of snowboarding, skateboarding, and mountain biking. Mountain boards look a little like a skateboard but have four large tires designed to roll over grass, rocks, and dirt.

Both recreational and competitive horseback riding are well established in Virginia. Every year, **steeplechase** fans watch to see who will win the Virginia Gold Cup Races. Virginia is also home to two NASCAR (National Association for Stock Car Auto Racing) tracks, located in Richmond and Martinsville. The tracks host stock-car races throughout the year.

There are more than 500 miles of hiking trails in Virginia's Shenandoah National Park.

QUICK FACTS

Richmond-born tennis player Arthur Ashe was the first African American to win the United States Tennis Open and the Wimbledon Men's Singles.

While Virginia has no professional sports teams, the many college teams attract spectators from around the state.

Basketball player Moses Malone, a native of Petersburg, went straight from high school to a 21-year professional basketball career in the American Basketball League and the National Basketball League (NBA). Malone is considered one of the best centers in the history of the NBA.

Brain Teasers

1

What natural force created Virginia's Blue Ridge Mountains?

a. the collision of tectonic plates

b. glaciers

c. volcanoes

d. an earthquake

Answer: c. Most of the rocks that form the Blue Ridge Mountains are more than 1 billion years old.

2

What is the official state folk dance of Virginia?

a. Square dance

b. Polka

c. Waltz

d. Highland dance

Answer: a. In 1991, the square dance was adopted as Virginia's official state folk dance.

3

What is Chincoteague Island known for?

Answer: Chincoteague Island is home to the only oyster museum in the world.

4

In which Virginia city did Patrick Henry make his "Give me liberty or give me death" speech?

Answer: Richmond. Patrick Henry was one of the leading patriots of the American Revolution.

5

What is the name of the area in the Arlington National Cemetery that is dedicated to soldiers who lost their lives in wartime and could not be identified?

Answer: The Tomb of the Unknown Soldier

6

Which of the following is the official state beverage of Virginia?

a. tea

b. coffee

c. grape juice

d. milk

Answer: d. Milk was adopted as the state beverage in 1982.

7

Which city in Virginia shares a name and main street with a city in Tennessee?

Answer: Bristol. Although joined by the same street, Bristol is actually two cities with two separate city governments.

8

Which Virginia island has had wild ponies since the 1600s?

Answer: Assateague Island has over 300 wild ponies. The island is divided between Virginia and Maryland.

FOR MORE INFORMATION

Books

Heilbroner, Joan. *Meet George Washington*. Landmark Books Series. New York: Random House Children's Publishing, 2001.

Leacock, Elspeth. *The Southeast: Travels Across America*. Washington, D.C.: National Geographic Society, 2002.

Sakurai, Gail. *The Jamestown Colony*. Chicago: Children's Press, 1997.

Web Sites

You can also go online and have a look at the following Web sites:

Commonwealth of Virginia
http://www.state.va.us/

Virginia On-line Travel Guide
http://www.virginia.org/

Traveler's Guide to Virginia
http://www.virginia.com/

Some Web sites stay current longer than others. To find other Virginia Web sites, enter search terms such as "Virginia," "Richmond," "Yorktown," or any other topic you want to research.

GLOSSARY

amphibians: animals that can live both on land and in water

archives: a collection of records and documents

bog: an area of wet, spongy ground

broiler chickens: chickens raised for their meat rather than their eggs

civilian: a person who does not work for the military or the police

commander in chief: supreme head of the armed forces

Constitutional Convention: the meeting in 1787 at which the Constitution of the United States was written

emancipation: the freeing of slaves

endangered: an animal or plant in danger of becoming extinct

Gross State Product: the value in dollars of goods and services produced in the state in one year

hijacked: an airplane, or other vehicle, seized by force

inducted: made a member of

metropolitan: relating to a large city or urban area

population density: the average number of people per unit of area

seceded: to have left an organization or nation

steeplechase: a horse race with obstacles such as ditches and hedges that the horse must jump over

threatened: an animal or plant whose numbers are declining so much that it may become endangered

transatlantic: crossing the Atlantic Ocean

Treaty of Paris: an agreement signed in Paris, where Great Britain acknowledged the independence of the United States

unanimously: agreed by everyone

veto: the power of a state leader to reject a bill passed by the legislature

INDEX